T0326124

RIGHT ON TRACK

TERRY DEARY

HORRIBLE HISTORIES.

COVER ILLUSTRATED BY
MARTIN BROWN

RIGHT ON TRACK

**READ
ALL
ABOUT
THE
NASTY
BITS!**

SCHOLASTIC

Published in the UK, 2022
Scholastic, Bosworth Avenue, Warwick, CV34 6XZ
Scholastic Ireland, 89E Lagan Road, Dublin Industrial Estate, Glasnevin, Dublin, D11 HP5F

SCHOLASTIC and associated logos are trademarks and/or registered trademarks of Scholastic Inc.

Text © Terry Deary, 2022
Illustrations © Martin Brown, 2022

The right of Terry Deary and Martin Brown to be identified as the author and illustrator of this work has been asserted by them under the Copyright, Designs and Patents Act 1988.

ISBN 978 0702 31235 9

Printed in UK
Paper made from wood grown in sustainable forests and other controlled sources.

3 5 7 9 10 8 6 4 2

www.scholastic.co.uk

WHAT'S INSIDE?

INTRODUCTION

History can be horrible. It can be cruel, and it can be unfair. In stories like Cinderella or Red Riding Hood the goodies win in the end. The cunning, the greedy and the wicked are the losers.

That doesn't happen in history. In real life the goodies can die in misery and the baddies end up rich and famous.

In railway history the good, the bad and the daft often came to horrible ends. But say 'thank you' to them all.

Why? Because railways are one of the world's safest ways to travel. And that's because when the good, the bad and the daft made mistakes the railways changed. In the past 200 years railways builders have learned.

If you want to build a railway you need a book that tells you how NOT to do it. How NOT to be blown up, scalded, crushed or cremated.

PUFFING PIONEERS

If you ever get a poor school report, you can explain to your angry adult...

THIS IS AWFUL. YOU ARE GROUNDED FOR 25 YEARS

BUT SOME OF THE CLEVEREST PEOPLE IN HISTORY HAD BAD SCHOOL REPORTS

SUCH AS?

RICHARD TREVITHICK

WHO?

ROTTEN FOR RICHARD

Who? Richard Trevithick was a Cornish tin miner. And Richard had been a bad pupil at his school in Cornwall. His teacher wrote:

> *Richard is a disobedient, slow, obstinate, spoiled boy, often absent and does not pay attention.*

The tin mines needed steam pumps to keep the mines free of water. They used pumps made by James Watt, a Scottish inventor.

Watt had a 'patent' on his steam engine. That means no one could use his invention without paying him a lot of money. Watt became very rich. It was like a jackpot Watt.

Mine owners, like Richard Trevithick, were fed up with paying the Scot a lot. Richard decided to make his own steam engine. But it would be high pressure. He wouldn't have to pay Watt.

That made the Scot Watt hot. Watt a fuss he made.

If that law had been passed, then railways would have been stopped in their tracks. History would be different. The government refused to pass that law. Not what Watt wanted.

The 'disobedient, slow, obstinate' young Richard was clever at maths and inventing. He began to make his high-pressure engines. They were smaller and lighter than Watt's low-pressure steam pumps. So disobedient, slow, obstinate Richard tried putting one on wheels. His first steam carriage, The Puffing Devil, ran on a road, not rails, in Cornwall, on Christmas Eve 1801.

It ran well enough but lasted as long as his family Christmas turkey. The steam car had no steering. On 28 December, it ran into a ditch. A local person took up the story:

The engineers went off to the hotel and made merry with a roast goose and drinks. They had forgotten the engine, as its water boiled away, the iron became red hot and the wood frame burned to a cinder.

Richard went on to build a high-pressure engine to power a corn mill in London. A boy was left in charge but stopped the engine without letting the steam out. It exploded and killed four people.

Of course, Watt said what?

I TOLD YOU SO

STEPHENSON STEAM-AND-SON

George Stephenson worked on Watts engines in a Newcastle coal mine, pumping out water.

He watched horses pull coal trucks along rails. He knew rails were a brilliant idea.

In 1821 he said that...

A horse on a common road can pull one ton. A horse on an iron road can pull TEN tons.

George Stephenson didn't invent the high-pressure steam engine. But when he saw the high-pressure engine of Richard Trevithick he made it work a bit better. He built a locomotive called *Blutcher*. It was good enough to pull coal trucks. He boasted...

My locomotive Blutcher *is worth FIFTY horses.*

If you know your fifty-times table that means a locomotive on an iron road could pull 500 tons. That was a bit of a fib. *Blutcher* could pull 30 tons up a hill at 4mph.

A STEAM LOCOMOTIVE WAS WORTH THIRTY HORSES?

NO A HORSE ON AN IRON ROAD CAN PULL TEN TONS SO BLUTCHER WAS WORTH THREE HORSES

George THEN started to plan railway lines that joined up the coal mines to the seaports near Newcastle. Stephenson's steam locomotives would pull the coal to the ships where it could be sold all around the world.

Edward Pease, a Darlington merchant, saw how good the Newcastle railways were. He wanted a railway line like the Newcastle ones from the Durham coalfields to the port of Stockton. He paid Stephenson to build it, but Edward had a great dream...

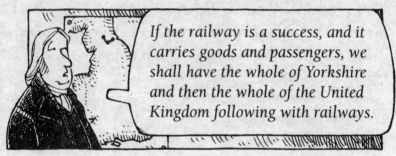

If the railway is a success, and it carries goods and passengers, we shall have the whole of Yorkshire and then the whole of the United Kingdom following with railways.

George Stephenson didn't 'invent' the railways – he took Pease's idea and made it work, just as he had with Trevithick's locomotive. George got all the praise...

GEORGE STEPHENSON, FATHER OF THE STEAM LOCOMOTIVE AND FATHER OF THE RAILWAYS

YOU ARE TOO KIND

Stephenson never said he was 'Father of the steam locomotive' – that was Trevithick. He never said he was 'Father of the Railways' – that was Pease. But George Stephenson never said he wasn't.

He WAS father of his son Robert Stephenson, and between them they went on to build railway lines all around the world.

Edward Pease thought his Darlington to Stockton line would be pulled by horses. But George told him...

Pease agreed. George planned the line while Robert built the locomotives. That first long railway was from the coal mines of Darlington to the seaport at Stockton. In 1825 that train carried something new ... people.

Crowds gathered to watch as George Stephenson's machine, *Locomotion No.1*, carrying 450 persons in 30 wagons at a speed of 15 miles (24km) per hour.

When the safety valve let out a screaming cloud of steam the crowds panicked. But *Locomotion* was not going to explode.

Around 450 people crowded into specially altered coal trucks and they set off. They had travelled a few hundred yards when one of the trucks came off the rails. It was lifted back on. Off they went for another few hundred yards and it happened again. The faulty truck was shunted off and a spectator was hurt.

The great train carried on for a few more miles … until *Locomotion No.1* itself broke down. A fouled valve.

There were 40,000 people waiting in Stockton for the (late) train which rolled in at 3:45 p.m. The great men and women of Stockton headed for the town hall where a banquet went on till midnight. They drank 23 toasts that night.

Faulty Truck

Imagine that. The world's first passenger train was an hour late. It wouldn't happen today.

BUT DID LOCOMOTION NUMBER ONE *REALLY* PULL AS MUCH AS 50 HORSES? 500 TONS?

SHHH THE DARLINGTON TO STOCKTON TRAIN COULD PULL JUST 88 TONS … BUT DON'T TELL ANYBODY

SHOCKING STEAM

James Watt said high-pressure steam was dangerous. In a way he was right. Use it carelessly and high-pressure steam can kill. But so can a match if you light it in the wrong place.

DO I HAVE MUCH PETROL IN MY TANK?

I'LL LIGHT A MATCH AND HAVE A LOOK...

BANG!

Steam engines, like matches, are safe if you use them properly.

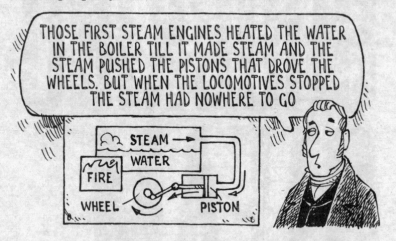

THOSE FIRST STEAM ENGINES HEATED THE WATER IN THE BOILER TILL IT MADE STEAM AND THE STEAM PUSHED THE PISTONS THAT DROVE THE WHEELS. BUT WHEN THE LOCOMOTIVES STOPPED THE STEAM HAD NOWHERE TO GO

STEAM →
WATER
FIRE
WHEEL
PISTON

Brunton's blast. Philadelphia, County Durham, England, 1815

One of the first steam locomotive explosions was the deadliest. Brunton's *Mechanical Traveller* was a steam engine with legs that pushed it along. He had it parked, steaming, near his house.

The *Mechanical Traveller* was so amazing the local people came out of their homes to wonder at it. But Brunton's boiler went bang. The driver was killed instantly (they usually were) while Brunton's nearby cottage was shattered. Mrs Brunton lived. Most of the victims were nosy neighbours.

Thirteen people died in this first disaster.

Safety sense

George Stephenson has a clever manager in his locomotive factory. The manager was called Timothy Hackworth. Hackworth came up with 'safety valves'.

But steam is power, steam is speed. Imagine you are a driver...

Dangerous drivers stopped the valve from working. It gave them more speed and power. Sometimes it worked, but sometimes...

SAFETY LAST

'Locomotion' loony. England, 1828

Everyone remembers *Locomotion* and the way it pulled the first passenger train in 1825. Hardly anybody remembers it was a killer. In 1828 the driver John Cree stopped *Locomotion* to take on water.

The gurgling and hissing of the water must have warned them that a disaster was coming. Timothy Hackworth said in his diary...

> ### JULY 1ST, 1828
> While John Cree was getting water at Aycliffe Lane with his assistant, Edward Turnbull, the engine exploded around one o'clock. He died on the 3rd at 3 o'clock in the morning.

And what happened to young assistant Edward Turnbull? Ed was scalded by the steam, but he survived with a face that was stained and scarred with soot-black speckles. He had to suffer bullying for the rest of his days.

Locomotion was treated a little more kindly. It was rebuilt.

Bottle blow. USA, 1831

Spotty Turnbull was a lucky fireman. The fireman on the American locomotive, *The Best Friend of Charleston*, was not so lucky.

Best Friend was a loco with a boiler that looked like a beer bottle. It could race along at 20 miles an hour. The Charleston Courier newspaper reported:

29 December 1830

The one hundred and forty-one persons flew on the wings of wind at the speed of fifteen to twenty-five miles per hour, defeating time and space, leaving all the world behind.

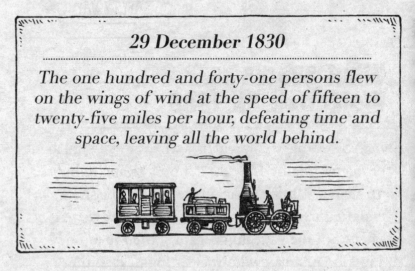

In 1831 the fireman had been shovelling coal all morning and stopped to eat his lunch as the boiler burbled away. The steam began to hiss and whistle (or wiss and histle) out of the safety valve. It really annoyed the fireman. So, he put a plank of wood on the safety valve ... and sat on it to finish his pie.

Steam could not get out of the top of the boiler so it blew apart the bottom. The driver was scalded but the fireman was blown into the air and died when he hit the ground.

What 'ave we ear?
Wolverton, UK, 1850

In Wolverton, 26 March 1850 there was a similar problem. Engine 157 was left on a siding to build up steam. When the steam was up to pressure it started to escape through the safety valve ... safely. But the squealing steam started to annoy a workman's mate who was sitting near to the locomotive. He screwed down the safety valves as tightly as he could.

The boiler exploded. The workman had his ear blown off.

Express-o coffee.
Brighton, UK, 1853

The driver of tank engine No.10 had been warned not to let his engine build up more than 80 pounds of pressure. The driver of No.10 screwed down the safety valve till it reached 100 pounds. Of course, it exploded. The roof of the nearby station was mostly destroyed, and the driver was just as splattered. You want to know, WHY would he do such a thing?

The driver had climbed on to the engine boiler to heat a can of coffee over the steam ... the higher the pressure the hotter the coffee.

Putrid poetry.
Bromsgrove Station, UK, 1840

Thomas Scaife and Joseph Rutherford of *The Birmingham and Gloucester Railway* died when an engine boiler exploded. The killer locomotive was named *Surprise*.

BIRMINGHAM
AND GLOUCESTER
~~RAILWAY~~
Scrap Metal Merchants

SURPRISE!
SALE NOW ON

~~One Railway Engine~~
Pile of Scrap Metal
Three shillings or nearest offer

The railway company was selling *Surprise* and the buyer was having a test-run. The wrecked engine was NOT sold. Surprise, surprise.

Scaife's headstone has a long and famous poem. It compares the dead man with a dead locomotive. How sweet.

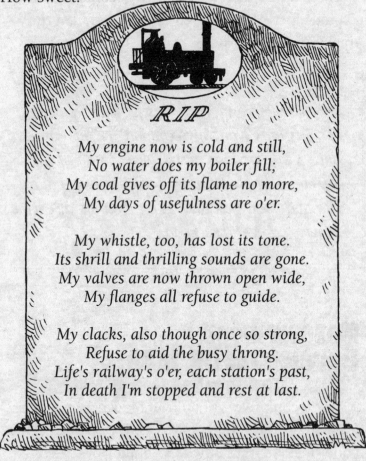

RIP

My engine now is cold and still,
No water does my boiler fill;
My coal gives off its flame no more,
My days of usefulness are o'er.

My whistle, too, has lost its tone.
Its shrill and thrilling sounds are gone.
My valves are now thrown open wide,
My flanges all refuse to guide.

My clacks, also though once so strong,
Refuse to aid the busy throng.
Life's railway's o'er, each station's past,
In death I'm stopped and rest at last.

His clacks are gone? Like a dead duck ... whose quacks are gone.

Legs and logs. Harlem Railroad, New York, USA, 1839

You may not be killed by a blast, but you could live to have horrible nightmares for life.

A New York locomotive came off the rails then exploded. Workers arrived to put it back on the track. The report said...

> *The chief engineer was blown to pieces – his legs went into Union Park, his arms onto a pile of logs on the other side of the avenue, and his head was split in two parts. His abdomen was also burst and his intestines scattered over the road.*

Moscow mess. Manchester, UK, 1858

A new locomotive was built in Manchester for the Russian railways. It exploded as it was tested. Three boiler-makers were killed. A young worker had been sent off to get a new tool from the shed next door. Lucky boy.

He heard the roar and looked at the scene of blast. He found body parts scattered around. These included a set of false teeth, a boot with a foot in it. Boilermaker James Carmichael was blown 70 metres over a canal, trailing guts until he smashed into a wall.

The mess that was left was stuck to the wall. A badly made boiler plate was blamed.

The luckiest – OR unluckiest – victim of that Manchester explosion had to be Thomas Forsyth. Tom had been hit by the first train to run on the Liverpool to Manchester service in 1829. He had a leg amputated and replaced with a cork one.

Thomas lived almost 30 years until that Russian locomotive blew up. He suffered a deep wound to his forehead through which his brains seeped out. A piece of iron had killed him instantly.

SAVAGE SURVEYS

People around the world heard about the Stockton and Darlington railway. Other towns and other countries wanted a railway of their own.

But the railways also had enemies ... deadly enemies...

If you are building a railway, you need a railway line. First you have to plan where you want to go.

Manchester in the early 1800s had the cotton mills rolling out cloth for the world ... tough and ugly places to work. Steam engines drove the cotton mills and the engines drove the people to keep up.

> Whilst the engine runs, the people must work — men, women and children are linked together with iron and steam. The animal machine is chained tight to the iron machine, which knows no suffering or weariness.

Report from James Kay, 1832

Liverpool brought in the raw cotton from across the seas. Manchester mills turned it into cloth. But Liverpool and Manchester were 30 miles apart.

I OWN A FACTORY IN MANCHESTER. I WANT TO SEND MY GOODS TO THE PORT AT LIVERPOOL WHERE THEY CAN BE SHIPPED AROUND THE WORLD

I'M A LIVERPOOL SHIP OWNER. I BRING IN STUFF FOR MY FRIEND IN MANCHESTER. I WANT HIM TO GET IT QUICKLY. LET'S GET THAT CLEVER GEORGE STEPHENSON TO BUILD US A RAILWAY

MANCHESTER
LIVERPOOL

But not everyone wanted to see that railway built. Goods were carried between Manchester and Liverpool on barges on canals.

It took 12 hours – trains would take under 2 hours. The rich people who owned the canals would lose their business. They hated the idea of a railway.

SAVAGED SURVEYS – ENGLAND

You know where your line is going? Now you need to walk along the route to decide the best place to lay the rails. This is called a 'survey'. The canal owners on the Manchester to Liverpool line plotted to stop the survey so the line could never be built.

THEY WILL BUILD A RAILWAY OVER MY DEAD BODY

OR OVER THE BODIES OF THE SURVEYORS, EH BOSS? HURR, HURR, HURR

The first man to plan a line in 1822 was William James. He set off to walk the route. It was dangerous...

 • Landowner Robert Bradshaw set out to stop him. William James had to pay a famous heavyweight boxer as his bodyguard. The fighter's job was to carry the survey tools, but he was beaten in a battle and the instruments destroyed.

BOXER GOT BEAT

 • Bradshaw told the coal miners that a railway line would harm their jobs, so the miners attacked William James's planners. (In fact, the railways would make the miners much better off.)

 • The scared surveyors tried working at night to fool the attackers. When the miners caught William James, they threatened to throw him down a mineshaft.

ATTACK AT THE STROKE OF MIDNIGHT

 • Farmers locked their gates against James and their farm workers were armed with shotguns and pitchforks. One of James's team was stabbed in the back with a pitchfork as he tried to run away.

• In the villages gangs of women and children mobbed the surveyors and threw stones, all the while screaming and swearing.

WOMEN AND CHILDREN: WHO NEEDS MEN?

• The attackers almost won. The survey was held up for months. That delay cost William James money and he ended up in prison because he couldn't pay his bills.

In 1837 James took a stagecoach across the snowy moors of Cornwall. He got chilly, contracted pneumonia and died.

IT WOULD HAVE BEEN WARMER ON A TRAIN

But the survey went ahead. George Stephenson 'borrowed' William's ideas and finished the Liverpool to Manchester line.

William James had also planned a line in Kent and Robert Stephenson 'borrowed' that one, just as the Stephensons had 'borrowed' Timothy Hackworth's steam locomotive ideas. And, like Timothy Hackworth, William James was one of the railway revolution's losers.

The Liverpool to Manchester line was opened in 1830. It was a huge success. Other countries wanted railway lines. But, just like the poor William James, there were dangers waiting for the brave people who did the surveys.

ROPE TRICK - USA

A plan was made to build a Denver to Rio Grande line. Two companies had fought over who would build it. Both sides hired gunfighters to defend their bits of the line. The famous lawman Bat Masterson saved his bullets at one fight.

When the arguments were over the line had to be planned. That was even more dangerous.

A YOUNG SURVEYOR HAD TO CLIMB DOWN A FACE OF A HIGH CLIFF. HE PUT ON A LEATHER BELT AND FASTENED IT TO A ROPE

SIX STRONG MEN HELD THE ROPE AND SWUNG HIM OVER THE 65 METRE DROP

ONE OF THE MEN NOTICED THE ROPE WAS RUNNING OVER A ROCK AS SHARP AS A RAZOR. THE ROPE WAS ALMOST SAWN IN TWO

THEY WENT TO HAUL UP THE SURVEYOR BEFORE IT WAS TOO LATE BUT IT WAS TOO LATE

THE ROPE WENT SLACK IN THEIR HANDS AS IT SNAPPED. ALL THEY HEARD WAS THE YOUNG MAN'S SCREAM, AND THAT CAME TO A SUDDEN STOP

AHHHHH

GOLD GRABBING – SOUTH AMERICA

In South America, a team of surveyors came across a city. The city should have been glad to have the railway, but the mayor was a greedy man. He said...

I WANT A CHEST OF GOLD NEXT TUESDAY OR I WON'T LET YOU ENTER THE CITY

WE'LL HAVE TO PAY HIM

A week later the surveyors returned on the Monday evening with a chest of gold. They had to guard the gold before they handed it over the next morning. They shut themselves up in a building and set a guard with rifles.

If there was a city newspaper it may have looked like this:

THE CITY NEWS

GOLD GRABBERS GET GOT

A fortune in gold arrived at the warehouse at the city gates last night. Night fell … but it didn't hurt itself. Moon-shadows crept across the road … but they made no sound. Out of the shadows slipped men with guns. The door to the treasure room was forced open. The guards inside opened fire.

The robbers fired back as they ran … they weren't expecting to be met with bullets. Some of the robbers fell. At dawn the guards stepped out and looked at the men they had killed. One of the bodies was … the mayor.

Voters will be told to elect a new mayor next week.

The previous mayor will not be running for re-election

The mayor's plan had been to steal the gold. The surveyors would moan that they'd been robbed, but they would have to fetch another fortune. So, the mayor would be paid twice.

A greedy but great plan. It wasn't the gold that spoiled it but the lead. The lead bullet that ended up in the mayor's back.

SURVEY SLAUGHTER – MEXICO

The Americans called railways railroads. Railroad builders crossed America with their lines from the Atlantic to the Pacific. One problem was that the land wasn't empty. Native Americans had lived there for thousands of years and they didn't like railways destroying their trails and driving away the wildlife they lived on.

If you go on the line through Mexico today, you might see four wooden crosses by the side of the line. Four surveyors had set out to mark the line for the builders. But they were set upon by the native Americans. They fired back with their rifles but one by one they fell. The crosses mark their graves.

The settlers from Europe took a terrible revenge, and in the end it was the native Americans who were almost wiped out as their lands were stolen.

And the native Americans had been right. The settlers WERE killing off the bison they lived on and that left the indigenous people to starve.

A writer in 1889 saw the last of the bison killed...

Thirty years ago, millions of the great animals lived on the plains. Huge herds roamed, safely. Many thousands have been ruthlessly killed every season for past twenty years or more by white hunters and tourists just for their skins and for sport. Their huge carcasses left to fester and rot, and their white skeletons to scatter over the deserts and lonely plains.

In the 1500s there had been over 25 million bison in America. In just one winter, 1872, a million and a half bison were put on trains and sent to the cities in the east to be slaughtered.

The US army moved across the land to protect the settlers from the natives. Their general said if they shot bison, they would starve the native people to death. So, the soldiers had a contest:

FORT HAYS AND WALLACE

The BISON SHOOTING CHAMPIONSHIP OF THE WORLD

None of this would have been possible without the railways. Hunters shot bison to feed the workers as they built the lines. Hunters arrived in trainloads. The trains would slow down on their routes while hunters would either climb aboard the roofs of trains or fire shots at herds through the open windows.

I'M COVERED IN SOOT

NEVER MIND, THERE'S A WASH-BISON DOWN BELOW

The railroad builders also wanted rid of bison herds because they could wander over tracks and damage locomotives that hit them. Hunters like 'Buffalo Bill' Cody became famous.

I CAN KILL OVER A HUNDRED ANIMALS A DAY

By the 1880s the bison were almost extinct. They were killed by the natives, the hunters, the settlers and the soldiers. But it was the railroad that made the slaughter possible.

BORNEO BLOODSHED – BRITISH NORTH BORNEO

Just like the Celts in Roman Europe, the Dayak people of Borneo believed in the magical power of the human head. They removed the heads of enemies and were known to the settlers from Europe as...

HEADHUNTERS

The Celts gave up collecting heads when they became Christian, and so did the Dayaks. But at the time when the railways were being laid across their lands the Dayaks were still hunting heads.

Of course, the people who suffered were the surveyors who went into the jungles without a map or an army to protect them.

In British North Borneo, a team of surveyors set out to plot a railway route. They didn't return. A few native servants escaped to report a massacre.

When the next team of surveyors set out, they were almost defeated by another terrible enemy – the jungle diseases.

Surveyors in the Amazon jungles suffered the same sort of disaster. They were killed by native Americans firing poison darts and their bodies stuck on poles, head down, for their railway friends to find.

WALTER'S WONDER WALL - CANADA

Some surveys had happy endings, of course.

In 1871 Walter Moberly was sent to survey a line across Canada and followed the Columbia River till it reached the Columbia Mountain Range. That's where he felt he met a solid block of mountains.

IT WAS WALTER WALL MOUNTAIN. BUT I KEPT GOING

IT WAS ME WHO KEPT GOING

For months he rode along the river valleys but there was no way through for a railway line.

JUST WHEN I WAS ABOUT TO GIVE UP THE WALTER WONDER HAPPENED

AND I WONDER WHEN SUPPER IS

He returned to camp one day, exhausted, and looked up to see an eagle soar across the valley and head for the mountains. It appeared to fly through them.

He didn't take his eyes off the place where the eagle had vanished, and he reached a narrow valley between two mountains that was perfect for a railway line.

He named it Eagle Pass and it's still called that today.

Walter became a Canadian rail legend. He was given the great honour of driving in the last track spike of the Canadian Pacific Railway to complete the 2,000-mile route.

Where did he drive in that spike? At Eagle Pass, of course, where else?

Walter died in 1915 but he was a little bitter. Another Canadian surveyor, Albert Rogers, discovered another pass and named it after himself – Rogers Pass. But he had been following the notes written by Walter – who didn't have a pass named after him. Walter said Albert PINCHED his path plan.

So, he didn't get a pass named after him.

Missing:
one pony.

Appearance:
very tired.

Likes:
oats and scritches.

REWARD

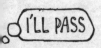

BRUTAL BUILDING

Now that you have some simple steam engines and you have surveyed your line, it is time to build it. The line needs to be as flat as you can make it.

VALLEYS AND RIVERS

When you come to a river valley, build a bridge. Just build it strong. Remember...

BAD BRIDGES BREAK

RIVER DEE BRIDGE, 1847

Even the great Robert Stephenson made mistakes. He built a bridge over the River Dee near Chester. Cast-iron can snap like a dry twig when it's bent. Wrought iron bends and stretches a little like toffee. Robert chose cast-iron. Oooops.

IT'S CHEAPER

Eight months after it was built an engine driver felt the line tremble under his locomotive as his train crossed. He was sure the bridge was about to collapse. He went faster and drove the locomotive to safety as a girder toppled into the River Dee below. The driver survived.

But the locomotive tender carrying the fuel and water was torn away along with the rest of the train. Three passengers died and so did the train guard and the fireman. Another nine were injured in the plunge.

The driver drove the locomotive to the next station to get help. Then he remembered that the next train would take a dive when it reached the broken girder. So, he headed back to warn them, and he saved more lives. A hero.

Nine injured in Dee plunge!

THE TAY BRIDGE, 1879

Thirty years later a l-o-n-g bridge was built over the River Tay in Scotland. What did Thomas Bouch use to build it?

On 29 December 1879 a storm broke. *Locomotive No.224* set off across the bridge. The signalman watched the train lights vanish into the night. A sudden gust clattered his cabin and he saw a flash of light from the bridge followed by blackness.

The signalman tried to walk the bridge for a closer look but he was blown back. He went down to the sheltered shore of the Tay and at that moment the moon broke through the clouds. It showed a mangled and tangled wreckage of girders. There was no train. Seventy-five people, including the train crew, went to feed the fishes. Only forty-six of the corpses were ever recovered.

The disaster is famous because of a terrible poem written by Scottish scribbler William McGonagall. McGonagall – who was NOT a bridge expert – added some advice in his ruin of rhymes:

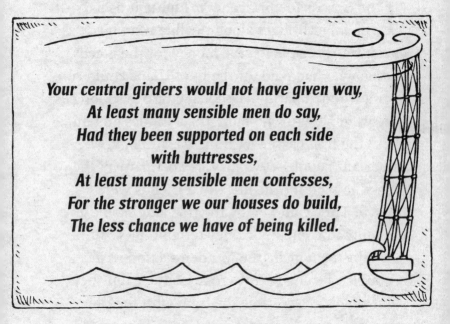

Your central girders would not have given way,
At least many sensible men do say,
Had they been supported on each side
with buttresses,
At least many sensible men confesses,
For the stronger we our houses do build,
The less chance we have of being killed.

Locomotive No.224 was hauled out and repaired. The sick Scottish railwaymen nicknamed it 'The Diver', though many drivers refused to take it over the new bridge. It kept on working for another 40 years.

The stone pillars that held the ruined old bridge can still be seen.

GASCONADE BRIDGE, USA, 1855

The Gasconade Bridge wasn't quite finished. All the other bridges along the line were made as cheaply as possible to save money for the greedy people who had paid for the line. Trains could run over a wooden part of Gasconade Bridge so long as they went slowly – no more than 4 miles an hour.

But the first passenger train was full of very important people – two mayors and many of the men who paid for the line. Rich friends were invited. They could enjoy the ride and maybe give the railroad company money to build more lines.

A rainstorm made the wooden section weak. A couple of trains went across safely … but they went slowly. Then came the train with the rich, important people. And it was LATE. That would never do. The driver sped up.

4 MILES AN HOUR? MORE LIKE 24 TO MAKE UP FOR LOST TIME

GOOD IDEA

Daft. Around forty people died, another 200 were injured and some of those died later from infected wounds. Two mayors and other top men died. Only two women were on the train – women were not considered to be very important people at that time (by men).

Rescue was slow but a lot of people did rush to the scene of the accident … to rob the rich of everything they had on them.

Greed caused the accident and greed enjoyed the result.

HILLS: MAKE A CUTTING

If your line meets a hill, then you may want to cut a groove in it rather than climb to the top. This is called a 'cutting' and you can guess why.

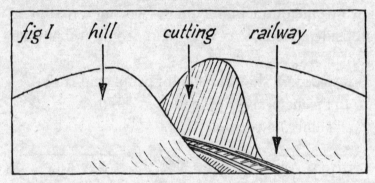

fig I   hill   cutting   railway

You have to move a terrific amount of soil to do this. And there were no steam or petrol machines to help the workers until the 1880s. The work was done by 'navigators' … known as 'navvies' for short – who were men strong enough to pick and shovel and dynamite all day long. The bosses thought each navvy should move 20 tons of earth each day. (That's three London buses.)

The problem was the deeper you went the more dangerous it became because the sides of the cutting could slide down and bury you.

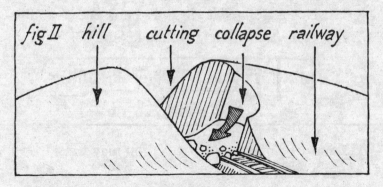

Some historians say there were three deaths for every mile of track that the navvies put down. One navvy claimed...

It was said that the workmen could lay nearly a full line made from injured men's legs.

IT RUNS FROM HIPPERHOLME...

TO BOOTLE

A man called John Kent died at Edge Hill. *The Liverpool Mercury* newspaper reported:

He was propping up a heavy bank of clay, fifteen feet high, when the mass fell upon him and literally crushed his bowels out of his body.

NOTE: This is a *Horrible Histories* book and it would NEVER come up with a terrible joke like this:

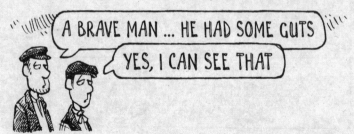

If you have any soil from the cutting you can use it to fill in a valley and keep your line flat. This is an 'embankment'.

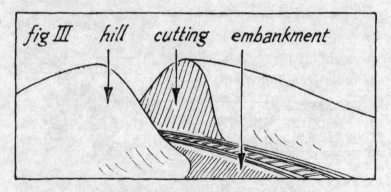

MOUNTAINS: DIG A TUNNEL

If a hill is too big to make a cutting, then dig a tunnel. Maybe the most dangerous job of all.

The Woodhead tunnel was under the Pennines in 1845. Most tunnels dug 'shafts' down from the top so the navvies could dig from the inside-out as well as the outside-in. Here's how it worked:

LOWER A BUCKET DOWN THE SHAFT BIG ENOUGH TO TAKE A SMALL TEAM OF WORKERS

LAY THE DYNAMITE AND LIGHT A FUSE THAT WILL TAKE A MINUTE TO BURN

LET THE WORKERS CLIMB INTO BUCKET. HAUL THEM BACK TO THE SURFACE TILL THE DYNAMITE HAS EXPLODED

LOWER THE WORKERS AND LET THEM SHOVEL THE LOOSE ROCK INTO THE BUCKET

And you'll have spotted the danger in the plan? Of course you did.

What happens if you light the fuse then the bucket gets stuck? It's nighty-night navvies.

In a tunnel in Wales twelve men and a boy died when the dynamite exploded too soon.
The inspector wrote:

> Two of the dead, Richard Parsons and the boy Clements, were blown to atoms; some small fragments only of their bodies having been found.

The 'atoms' of John Clements were just 13 years old. But don't worry about the little children. A law called the 'Mines Act' of 1842 banned the use of children under the age of 10.

SMOKY DEATH

If you finish your tunnel without killing too many navvies, you should leave their shafts to let out the smoke from the old steam trains.

In 1944 Italy was at war and food was short. People crowded on to the trains to get to the farms in the countryside to take food back to the hungry cities. The passengers would end up dead rich … rich, or dead. The trains were overloaded.

One train entered the Balvano tunnel. That tunnel had no shafts.

WE JUST LET THE WIND BLOW THROUGH THE TUNNEL, AND IT CLEARS OUT THE SMOKE

But one night there was no wind. A locomotive entered the tunnel then started to skid on the wet track. The smoke built up in the tunnel and began to choke the 600 passengers. The driver tried to reverse back out, but he fell to the floor, poisoned by the gases.

Some of the passengers at the back of the train were near the entrance to the tunnel. They struggled out and collapsed on the lines. The rescue train couldn't get in without running over them.

510 died and 90 were ill with gas poisoning.

Quick question: What did the Italian Railway chiefs do to stop this happening again?

a)   They had shafts dug to let out smoky air

b)   They only let trains enter Balvano tunnel on windy days

c)   They did nothing

Answer: (c)

DID YOU KNOW...

Victorians were worried that dark tunnels were the perfect place for criminals to attack. One woman said a strange man tried to kiss her in a tunnel but even worse...

Other women began to hold pins between their lips to protect themselves from wicked kissers. That must have needled the men.

THE WATFORD TUNNEL DISASTER

The railways line at Watford didn't really need a tunnel. The line could have run across the land owned by the Earl of Essex. But the Earl did NOT want to spoil the quiet view from his home. George Stephenson had to build a tunnel. It was through dangerous ground and would cost a lot of money. But his Lordship refused to allow trains to cross his land.

In 1838 the tunnel collapsed and killed 60 navvies.

SAD. BUT AT LEAST MY VIEW HAS NOT BEEN SPOILED

GEELONG RAILWAY BRIDGE ACCIDENT

Passing under a bridge could be as dangerous as a tunnel. In June 1857, the town of Geelong, Australia, planned a party to welcome the new railway. A train set off full of important passengers.

The party in Geelong was waiting with...

- three tons of poultry
- three tons of meats
- one ton of fish
- one ton of pastries
- half a ton of jellies and ices
- half a ton of fruit
- a ton of bread
- and a lake of wines, spirits and ales.

How much of this feast did the important passengers on the first train eat? Nothing.

The train was late. A local newspaper reported...

27 June 1858

ENGINEER'S END

The Geelong & Melbourne Railway Company's first trip started with high hopes and ended in disaster.

The first train started at half-past ten, taking important persons and six hundred others. The train went at an easy rate till it neared Cowie's Creek. Then Mr Henry Walters, head of locomotives for the company, was standing on the engine looking backwards. He did not notice the wooden bridge under which the line passes so his head came into contact with one of the beams.

He was struck on the head and stunned. As he fell off the engine his head again struck against the iron steps of the first carriage and the corner of the post. The train was at once stopped and the unlucky man picked up.

Mr Walters

Doctors hurried to help him, but the poor fellow had received such severe injuries in the head and spine that there was no hope. He was taken to town with the greatest care, but he died later that afternoon. This sad accident cast a gloom over the people who heard of it.

The timbers of the bridge were just 40cm from the carriage sides when most railways are at least twice as much.

Arriving in Geelong

By the time the important people reached Geelong the 4,000 townsfolk had eaten the entire ten tons of food.

ENGINEER'S END 2

Even retired engineers could die on their railways. George Churchward was the Chief Engineer of the Great Western Railway from 1902. He had retired in 1922 but lived close to his lovely Great Western Railway at Swindon. He was half blind and deaf by 1933 when he went to check a line fault near his home. He didn't see (or hear) the express that hit him.

GREAT WESTERN RAILWAY

GEORGE CHURCHWARD

Former Chief Engineer
of this fine railway

Born
31 January 1857

Died
19 December 1933

Flattened but not forgotten

DID YOU KNOW...

By the end of the 1800s the railways of Britain cost another £1,000 a mile (or £200,000 in today's money). That was just to pay for beer for the navvies.

PAINFUL FOR PASSENGERS

You have your railway built with tunnels and embankments, cuttings and bridges. Now you need engines and coaches – trains – to run on those lines.

The Stephensons had built the Liverpool to Manchester line but passengers would not want to be tugged along by feeble locomotives like *Locomotion No.1*. They wanted the best of the best locomotives. The owners of the line set up a competition to find out who had the best steam locomotives. They held...

THE RAINHILL TRIALS

There were five engines that entered the trials to decide who was best.

5 Cycloped

It was worked by a horse trotting along a treadmill. The horse fell through the belt and broke it,  but the machine should never have entered as the rules said a steam locomotive. Some historians think the *Cycloped* was designed as a joke to entertain the crowds. The *Cycloped* withdrew. Then there were 4...

New Cocoa-motive Hot Chocolate

With an intense, smoky flavour, it will transport you right to the land of nod

4 Novelty

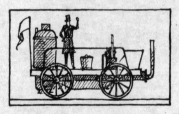

Novelty's builders heard about the contest just seven weeks before it happened and threw together a machine from bits of London fire-engines. It was described as a 'tea urn' by people who saw it. Its air pumps burst and it didn't complete the competition. Two down, three to go...

3 The Perseverance

It didn't persevere. It was built in Edinburgh by a company that made steam coaches. A cheeky Scottish worker had slipped into the Stephensons' factory in Newcastle and started asking about the locomotives. He was thrown out. Spying was clearly part of the game. The red wheels were damaged as it was unloaded at Liverpool but it was never fast enough.

2 The Sans Pareil

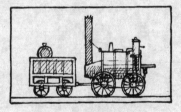

This was Timothy Hackworth's effort. He had to work long days for the Stephensons. He worked nights on his *Sans Pareil*. He had no time to test his locomotive. *Sans Pareil* could have won, but it had faulty valves and failed the trial. It might have been faster and more powerful than Robert Stephenson's Rocket. So then there was one...

1 Rocket

The sunflower-yellow boiler was topped with a white chimney. Smart as paint. The Stephensons had taken Hackworth's ideas and improved them. *Rocket* won the contest and was there when the line opened in 1830.

ROCKET MAN DOWN

On the great day of the opening 15 September 1830, eight trains ran, side by side, on the two lines to Manchester. The famous Duke of Wellington rode in one train. William Huskisson, member of parliament, was in another one of the trains. The locomotives stopped for water.

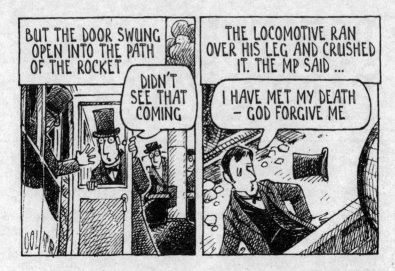

Huskisson was rushed to hospital in Manchester, but he then died. He is famous for being the first passenger killed on the railways. BUT...

DID YOU KNOW...

At Eaglescliffe, near Stockton, an old report says that in 1827...

An unnamed female – thought to be a blind beggar – was killed by the steam machine on the railway.

That was two years before Huskisson's death. So, Huskisson is famous for something he was not. He was NOT the first victim. (Maybe.)

PITY THE PASSENGERS

The first years of the railways were dangerous. The train companies learned from their mistakes … but passengers died. Would YOU like to be a passenger on an early railway?

CORRIDORS

No one had the idea of carriages with a corridor joining them. So, a train guard would have to check tickets by walking along the step-boards outside of the carriages and punch tickets through the carriage windows. Thomas Port was a guard on the Euston train to Birmingham and set off along the step-boards. The tricky bit was crossing from one carriage to the next. He slipped and fell under the wheels. The doctors amputated his legs (without an anaesthetic), but he died from loss of blood.

WINDOWS

Early carriages had no glass in the windows, so the clothes of the passengers were in danger of being holed by hot sparks. Showers of cinders could burn them bald. In time windows were fitted – but only in first class, as you would expect. In the Czech Republic in 1845, the railway engineer Jan Perner leaned out of his carriage to look at the railway he had helped to build. He was struck by a careless passing pole. He died the next day. Windows save whacks.

SIGNALS

There were no signals on the first railway tracks, and they were single lines. If one train met another head-to-head, then one of them went into reverse ... but crashes happened. On some lines there was a policeman who would time the trains. If the train broke down, he would have to run to the end and stop following trains. The drivers were told to build a coal fire in the middle of the track to give warning to following trains. Smoke signals in fact.

DOORS

Passengers were too fond of getting out for a short break on long journeys – or jumping on or off between station stops. The answer? Have the guard come along and lock all the doors before the train set off. In 1836 a broken axle sent a carriage tumbling down an embankment – with passengers trapped like baked beans in a can. Luckily the coach didn't catch fire and turn them in to baked beings ... and amazingly no one was seriously hurt. But locking in passengers would soon be banned.

COUPLINGS

Locos and coaches were joined by chains. As the locomotive went faster or slower the crashing of coach on coach shook the passengers. A young fireman was sent to uncouple coaches on his train. Two trucks came together. His head was crushed, and he suffered train-chain brain-drain damage.

BRAKES

The early locomotives, like *Rocket*, had no brakes. After the Huskisson death in 1830, brakes were fitted on locomotives and carriages, but they were not very good. Trains would take around half a mile to come to a halt.

Then, in 1889, carriages with poor brakes ran back down a slope at Armagh, Ireland. They crashed with the next train to come along. Eighty passengers died. Many were children on a Sunday-school trip. The law said better brakes had to be fitted – that law only took 60 years after the *Rocket* disaster.

WARNINGS

In 1833 on the Leicester and Swannington Railway, a Robert Stephenson loco called *Samson* collided with a horse and cart loaded with butter and eggs. They were scrambled. The engine had a horn, toot-toot, but it seems it was not loud enough. The line manager, Mr Bagster, came up with the idea for the first steam whistles.

FOOD

Before the days of food on trains, passengers had to get off at stations to buy food or drink for themselves. But this slowed the journey and cost the railway companies money. A report said...

> *It is a nuisance, selling of Eccles Cakes and Ale to passengers at almost every stop between Warrington Junction and Manchester.*

CLASSES

There were carriages with no roofs and bench seats for 'third-class' passengers. Second class were covered and rich people paid extra for comfy first class.

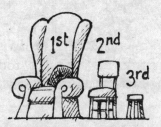

73

DID YOU KNOW...

The rich didn't expect to share with 'lower' class people. In India, Sir Ashutosh Mukherjee was a rich lawyer who dozed off in a first-class carriage. A British landowner got on the train and thought he should not share with an Indian. Ashutosh woke to find that the landowner had thrown his slippers out of the window. The British man then fell asleep and woke to find his jacket was missing.

WHERE'S MY JACKET?

OH YOUR JACKET? IT HAS GONE TO FETCH MY SLIPPERS

EMERGENCY CORD

Trains have emergency handles. Pull the handle if there is a problem and the driver will get the message and stop. Great idea. But in the 1830s someone came up with a daft way to work it.

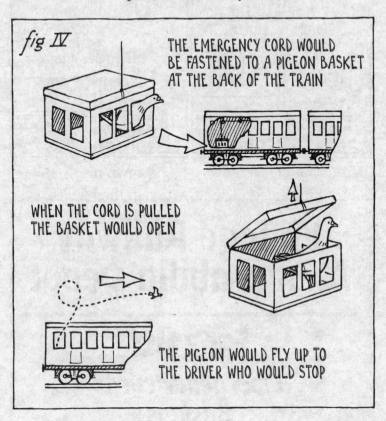

fig IV

THE EMERGENCY CORD WOULD BE FASTENED TO A PIGEON BASKET AT THE BACK OF THE TRAIN

WHEN THE CORD IS PULLED THE BASKET WOULD OPEN

THE PIGEON WOULD FLY UP TO THE DRIVER WHO WOULD STOP

Then someone said...

BUT THE TRAIN IS SO FAST THE PIGEON CAN'T OVERTAKE IT AND REACH THE DRIVER

A later idea was to fasten the cord to a drumstick that bashed a gong when it was pulled.

It was tried but the sound was blown away.

DEADLY DISEASES

Indian illness

Accidents killed railway builders. But diseases killed many more. The owners of a line found this a bit annoying. Dead annoying. But not so dead as the poor workers.

In building the Ghat line 42,000 workers were given jobs. 25,000 died, mostly from disease. More than half. That is a little bit more deadly than the Black Death was in the 1300s. But an angry boss complained...

DID YOU KNOW...

The British bosses tried to force the Indian workers to work the British way. The Indians carried baskets of rubble on their heads. A British master ordered the workers to use wheelbarrows. The Indians simply picked up the barrows and carried them on their heads.

Panama pain

A railway was built across Panama – that's the narrow bit between North America and South America. It was even more deadly than India.

In 1863 there were 800 Chinese men hired to build a line. They were paid so little they were no more than slaves. Their lives were so bad there were many who wanted to die. Some paid friends to chop off their heads while others tied stones to their feet and jumped in the river.

Irish navvies came to help. They were used to building railways, but they suffered too, from...

• Deadly diseases: malaria, cholera, dysentery, smallpox

• Cruel creatures: savage snakes, alligators, poisonous insects.

Fifty American engineers went out in summer. Only two were still alive by Christmas.

Burying bodies in the swamps was tricky. But hospitals around the world needed corpses for student doctors to practise on. The Panama bodies were packed into barrels of pickle and sent off to medical schools around the world. The money that was made paid for the railway hospital.

Visit

PHENOMENAL PANAMA!

GORGEOUS WEATHER AND BEAUTIFUL TRAIN RIDES!

Just try to avoid the exotic creatures and diseases...

AWFUL FOR ANIMALS

Your railway is up and running. It is safe for human passengers. But what about animals? There have been some strange tales told. Can you learn from the history of railways? Take this quick test:

EXPRESS QUIZ

Simply answer (a), (b) or (c)

1 Rails are usually laid on wooden 'sleepers'. Sleepers in South Africa were made from steel, not wood. Why?
a) Wood snapped when elephants walked across the line
b) Wooden sleepers grew weak because lions sharpened their claws on them
c) White ants chewed the wooden sleepers to make their homes

IT'S NOT YOUR FAULT IT WAS WEAKENED BY LIONS AND ANTS

CRACK

2 In the 1880s Australian railways were built with the help of which animals?
   a) Kangaroos
   b) Camels
   c) Koala bears

3 You can still see 'Station Jim' at Slough in Berkshire. Jim is a dog. How long has he been there?

a) Over 5 years

b) over 25 years

c) Over 125 years

4 South African Signalman Edwin Wide had a helper to switch the points at Uitenhage train station. Who helped him?

a) Jack the Baboon

b) Ellie the Elephant

c) Penelope the Parrot

IT'S MY TURN

5 The Hachiko railway line in Japan is named after an Akita dog born in 1923. What did Hachiko do?

a) Rescued a baby that had fallen onto the track in the path of an express train

b) Waited for his master to get off the train long after his master had died.

c) Broke the world record by widdling on 973 telegraph poles on the line.

6 US farmers started putting cattle food between the tracks of the railway lines and the cows stood there eating it. Why did the farmers do that?
a) To stop the trains so the farmers could jump on board
b) To stop the trains so the cows could get to market
c) To kill the cows.

Answers:

1c The white ants eat wood and then use their poo to make the ant nest. Wooden you like to try that?

2b 1880s Western Australia wanted to connect with the other states but had to cross miles of dry lands. So, they used a dozen camels to survey the route. Five camels to ride on and the rest to carry what the surveyors needed. Water was so short the camels were only allowed to drink once every five days.

3c Jim was a dog used to collect money from passengers to give to the poor. He was taught to bark when money was put in his box. He could sit up and beg or lie down and 'die' take a bow or stand up on his hind legs. Passengers could see him sit on a chair, a pipe in his mouth and cap on his head. Station Jim died with his box on the platform in 1896 and his body was stuffed. If you can find

Slough Station, Jim is still there.

4a In 1880, in South Africa, railwayman Edwin Wide lost his legs in an accident and needed help to work the signals. He saw a clever baboon, Jack, in a market and bought him to push his wheelchair to the signal box where he worked. Jack learned to sweep floors and take out rubbish. The trains used their whistles to send messages to Edwin's signal box. Baboon Jack soon learned the whistles and began to pull the levers to change the points himself. Jack worked the signal-box for nine years without ever making a mistake.

5b Hachiko was the pet of Hidesaburo Ueno, a professor. Every day Ueno and Hachiko would walk together to the Shibuya train station, where Ueno would get on the train to work. Hachiko spent the day waiting for Ueno to come back. He did this for several years until, one day, Ueno never came home from work, as he had died. Of course, Hachiko went on waiting for his master's return. Every day the train would appear, so would Hachiko, searching for Ueno. Hachiko waited for more than nine years for his owner to return. Finally, one morning, in 1935, Hachiko was found dead. His body was stuffed and kept at the National Science Museum of Japan in Tokyo while a statue stands at the station. Still waiting.

6c American locomotives had metal bars along the front to push animals out of the way. They were called 'cow-catchers', but the truth is they were cow killers. Every time a cow was killed the railway company would pay the farmer good money for the dead animal. An old cow was worth very little at market, so the farmers let them stray into the paths of the trains. But the train companies found out and started to pay HALF as much money. The angry farmers went to war with the Michigan Central line, putting blocks on the lines, burning stations, messing with points, and even throwing stones at trains. The railway companies put a spy into the wrecking group and a dozen farmer-plotters went to jail.

CATTLE-RANCHER, TRAIN-WRECKER, JAIL-BIRD

Score:

5 or 6 – You're an ace railway driver.

3 or 4 – maybe you'll make a fireman.

1 or 2 – I hope you don't drive my train.

JUMBO VET, 1885

If a train hits a cow, it usually kills the cow. If a train hits an elephant, it usually kills the train. It happened in 1885.

You may guess it took place in Africa … but I guess you'd guess wrong. Because it happened in Ontario, Canada. The Barnum and Bailey Circus was in town and a dwarf Asian elephant called Tom Thumb was crossing the line on his way back to its animal carriage. An express goods train hit Tom and threw him down the bank, breaking his leg.

But the driver had thrown the engine into reverse. It shot backwards … and hit the world-famous African elephant, the massive 'Jumbo'. Jumbo died and the engine was wrecked.

Jumbo's skin was stuffed and put on show, but it was destroyed in a fire in 1975. His ashes were kept in a Peter Pan Crunchy Peanut Butter jar … the jumbo size, of course.

DERBY

Peter Pan

PEANUT BUTT

CRUNCH

YOU COULD ALMOST SAY I WAS A TRAINED ELEPHANT

SPOT THAT STRAY, 1838

Stray farm animals were a problem in the early days of railways. In Britain, a train company hired a man to sit on the roof of a carriage and look ahead with a telescope … through showers of soot and sparks. It was such a boring job the spotter soon grew tired and gave up. The railway company dropped the idea.

SPOTS OF SOOT AND ASH SPOTTING THE SPOTTER

SPOT SPOTS THE SPOTTED SPOTTING SPOTTER

DREADFUL DISASTERS

A train disaster can be a disaster for the owners of the railway. Passengers will stop travelling on your trains and you will run out of money. Even the Stephensons had accidents, but they didn't OWN the railways, so they kept going.

Learn from the Dreadful Disasters of other people and try not to make the same mistakes.

Collect tokens for a
FREE RIDE ON THE SLOWCOMOTIVE HERITAGE LINE

1   2   3   4   5

Bo'ness, Scotland, 1874

TWO express trains were due to pass through Bo'ness. The first one was eight minutes late so the dozy signalman thought it was the second (and last) one. In that case the main line would be clear. He let a goods train to shunt trucks onto the main line. Then he heard the second express roaring down the line. Oooops. He threw the signal to red to stop the train. The express driver's last words said it all.

Driver Robert Allen cried out to his fireman...

BRAKES! BRAKES! THAT IS A RED BUT IT'S TOO LATE

The driver and 15 passengers were killed. A road bridge was struck and so badly damaged it had to be demolished.

Lesson: hire signalmen with a brain ... or give the signal job to a baboon.

Round Oak, England, 1858

A train trip was planned from Wolverhampton to Worcester and back. It was a children's treat and around 750 packed in. But another 750 adults jumped on for the ride.

Back in the brake-van the guard, Cook, sat with

six friends. They were not allowed to be there. He began to show off with a silly trick: put the brake on when the train is moving, and all the carriages shake till the passengers' teeth rattle. Guard Cook's mates did this so many times the chains linking the carriages snapped. He patched them up at the next station and on they went.

But the patch wasn't strong enough. The overloaded train reached the top of a hill, the chains snapped, and 17 coaches rolled back down the hill, faster and faster.

Where was Cook with his brake? When he saw his carriages running downhill, he cried out...

JUMP! JUMP OR WE'LL ALL BE KILLED

Guard Cook jumped and saved his own skin. Then the runaway carriages reached the following train the mighty smash killed 14 people while 50 had serious injuries. Many were children.

Cook said he had put the brake on, but tests showed that he lied.

Lesson: don't overcrowd your train ... or give the train-guard job to a baboon. (A baboon that has no friends.)

Abergele, North Wales, 1868

A careless brakesman forgot to put the brakes on a goods train that had been parked. It ran off down the main line towards Abergele. The Irish Mail train was heading towards the runaway trucks.

Arthur Thompson, the engine driver of the Irish Mail, saw the runaway wagons and shut off steam. Thompson then prepared to jump off and called to his fireman...

For God's sake, Joe, jump; we can do no more.

But it was no-go for Joe. Thompson jumped; his fireman did not. Thompson heard his mate's desperate cry, the deafening collision, but then ... no other human sound.

A bit like the Round Oak tragedy? No, much worse.

The runaway wagons were carrying 50 wooden barrels with 8,000 litres of paraffin oil. They sprayed over the Irish Mail coaches and caught fire. Everyone in the front four carriages died along with fireman Joe.

A passenger in one of the back coaches lived. He was the Marquis of Hamilton and said...

I jumped out of the carriage when a fearful sight met my view. Already the three passenger carriages were covered in dense sheets of flame and smoke.

It happened in an instant. Not a sound, not a scream, not a struggle to escape, or a movement of any sort in the doomed carriages.

It was as if the burning carriages were empty of passengers.

The doors to each compartment were locked. There were thirty-three passengers inside. Not one survived. An accident report said later...

They can only be described as charred pieces of flesh and bone.

Lesson: don't lock passengers in the carriages ... or give the brakesman job to a baboon.

Norton Fitzwarren, England, 1890

Norton Fitzwarren is a village on the Great Western rail line.

The villain of this disaster was George Rice, a signalman. He sat alone in his lonely box, through a freezing November night, with dreams of a warm bed. A fast London train was headed down the London line, so he moved a slow goods train onto the Exeter Line.

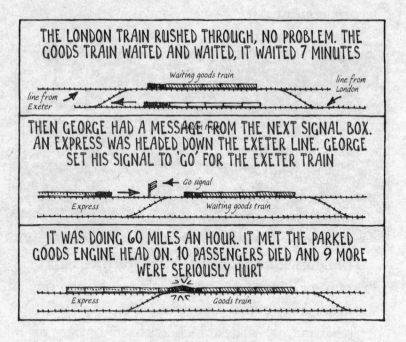

THE LONDON TRAIN RUSHED THROUGH, NO PROBLEM. THE GOODS TRAIN WAITED AND WAITED, IT WAITED 7 MINUTES

Waiting goods train

line from London

line from Exeter

THEN GEORGE HAD A MESSAGE FROM THE NEXT SIGNAL BOX. AN EXPRESS WAS HEADED DOWN THE EXETER LINE. GEORGE SET HIS SIGNAL TO 'GO' FOR THE EXETER TRAIN

Go signal

Express

Waiting goods train

IT WAS DOING 60 MILES AN HOUR. IT MET THE PARKED GOODS ENGINE HEAD ON. 10 PASSENGERS DIED AND 9 MORE WERE SERIOUSLY HURT

Express

Goods train

And the b-i-g question was, 'Why did George Rice signal the fast train forward when the goods train was parked on its line?'

Because he forgot it was there. George tried to explain...

I WAS KNOCKED OVER BY A TRAIN 10 MONTHS AGO AND I'VE NEVER BEEN RIGHT SINCE. I'D BEEN BAD IN THE HEAD ALL NIGHT

Lesson: don't let signalmen work after they've been hit on the head … or give the signal job to a baboon that hasn't been knocked on the head.

The Staplehurst Rail Crash, 9 June, 1865

The Staplehurst disaster was a railway accident in Kent, England. Ten passengers died and forty more were injured. One of the most famous men in England was on that train. He was the writer Charles Dickens. He was a Victorian celeb, travelling back from a holiday in Paris with his girlfriend, Ellen, and her mother.

As the happy couple puffed through Kent, disaster struck. Workmen had taken up the track over a wooden bridge. The track-repair boss read the timetable and thought there would be no trains that day.

The train ran out of rails, it juddered and the engine crunched over a low bridge which collapsed. Most of the following carriages followed the engine into the stream bed. Charles Dickens was in a carriage at the back. It tipped but didn't fall. He was one of the first to recover his wits. He wrote in a letter to his friend…

I was in the only carriage that did not go over into the stream. It hung suspended and balanced in an apparently impossible manner. Two ladies were my fellow passengers; an old one, and a young one. The old lady cried out 'My God!' and the young one screamed.

I caught hold of them both. The young lady said in a frantic way, 'Let us join hands and die friends.'

Of course, the passengers were locked in. Once the guard freed him Dickens helped his Ellen out of the carriage, along with her mother, then set about rescuing other passengers. It was grim work.

Suddenly I came upon a staggering man covered with blood (I think he must have been flung clean out of his carriage) with such a frightful cut across the skull that I couldn't bear to look at him. I poured some water over his face, and gave him some brandy to drink, and laid him down on the grass. He said, 'I am gone,' and died afterwards.

There were no great expectations that the injured man could live.

Then I stumbled over a lady lying on her back against a little tree, with blood streaming over her face (which was the colour of lead). Her blood ran in a number of little streams from the head. I asked her if she could swallow a little brandy, and she just nodded, and I gave her some and left her for somebody else. The next time I passed her, she was dead.

They were hard times. She wouldn't get to sing another Christmas carol or boast...

A man pinned under the carriage was one of the ten to die. Ellen was one of the 40 injured. Dickens worked for three hours helping where he could and he was called a hero. But the memory of the crash never left him.

In writing these few words of my memories, I feel the shake and am forced to stop.

For the rest of his life Dickens tried not to travel by express trains, and even suffered terrors when he was on slow train services. He sometimes got off several stops before his destination and walked the rest of the way.

The Staplehurst accident happened in 1865 on 9 June. Charles Dickens died five years later in 1870 … on 9 June.

Dying on the day of the disaster? Was that a spooky chance?

Lesson: make sure line workers know how to read a timetable … or (you guessed it) give the track-laying job to a baboon. (A baboon who can read.)

OTHER MISTAKES

The St-Hilaire, Canada, 1864

The train headed for a swing bridge that was open to allow barges to pass through. The red light on the railway tracks said 'Stop' … but the driver said 'Go' and plunged his train into the river. The barge was crushed, and 99 people on the river and on the train were drowned.

Saint-Michel-de-Maurienne, France, 1917

It was the First World War and a train-load of French troops were heading home from fighting in Italy. The soldiers survived the fighting, but the train went downhill too fast and didn't have good enough brakes to slow down. The carriages came off the rails and caught fire. The soldiers were carrying bombs that exploded in the flames. There were 675 people who died. It is France's most deadly rail accident.

THE DAFTEST TRAIN DISASTERS

Texas, USA, 1896

Imagine if you could watch two trains crash and explode … and no one was hurt. What fun. People would pay to see that and 30,000 did pay when the showman William Crush set it up.

Two six-car trains of old engines and wagons were set to crash, head-on, at a painted, wooden mock-station. The engines collided and their boilers exploded like a bomb. Like a bomb they sent metal flying everywhere. Many people were injured and three died. What a show, what fun.

India, 1917

A passenger train came across some damaged track. A messenger was sent to the next town to fetch a repair team. But the crew on the passenger train managed to repair it and set off again, full steam ahead.

They collided head-on with the train that was being sent to help them.

STEAMING SPOOKS

SEND YOUR **SPIRITS SOARING** ON THE **GREAT SOUTHERN RAILWAY**

If your railway is up and running then do NOT tell your passengers ghost stories or they may never travel on your trains again. Don't tell them spooky tales like...

THE NEWMARKET ARCH CRASH – 6 JUNE, 1851

M r Dickens was not the only victim of the bad-day curse.

On 6 June 1851, a train was running between Brighton and Lewes when it struck a sleeper that had been laid across the track. A gang of workers were in the area, leaving sleepers at the side of the track, but the nearest worker was a few hundred yards away. The train came off the rails and fell onto the road killing two crew and three passengers.

The main suspect was little Jimmy Boakes who lived in a cottage alongside the track. The police grilled little Jimmy for hours, but the boy denied it...

IT WASN'T ME, GUV AND, ANYWAY, HOW COULD A TEN-YEAR-OLD BOY LIFT A 3-METRE SLEEPER?

TRUE YOU'D HAVE TO USE A LEVER OF SOME SORT

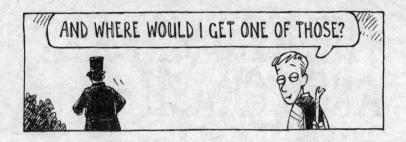

AND WHERE WOULD I GET ONE OF THOSE?

An unsolved mystery. But … on 6 June 1852, one year later to the day, little Jimmy went again to view the scene of the accident. He was struck by a bolt of lightning and killed.

Bad luck? Or Jimmy's doom? A spooky railway justice?

'ZANETTI', ITALY, 1911

In the summer of 1911, a train from Rome set off with three carriages and 106 passengers. It should have gone through a mountain tunnel in Lombard, Italy. It is said that the train entered the half-mile tunnel, but it never came out.

Dozens of people had seen the train leave the station in Rome and enter the tunnel. There were two passengers found who said they'd jumped off the train just before it vanished. They said that the passengers had been terrified when the train was covered with milky mist which gradually became thicker.

Was a whole train kidnapped by aliens? Or had it entered a time portal and gone back in time? Since that day in 1911 dozens of people around the world have said they have seen the ghost train.

In 1926 a relative of one of the lost passengers read a report from Mexico:

2 June 1845
Mexican Rail Mystery

This week a railway train showed up in the country and stopped. Out stepped 104 passengers who said they were from Italy. Clearly these people were mad and have been locked away in a home for lunatics.

1845? It appeared 66 years before it disappeared and halfway across the world? Time travel? And where is the train now? Still zipping around the world?

Many years later, the train appeared again in Europe. In 1955 an old-fashioned train appeared not far from Zavalichi in Ukraine. The signalman saw it moving without a sound.

The ghost train has been seen several times in countries such as Russia, India, Germany, Italy and Romania. In Eastern Russia a witness said the train ran into a flock of hens.

Then in 1991 a scientist was investigating ghostly happenings and jumped onto the train. He has never been seen since.

Beware next time you go to a fairground...

A true terror? Or hogwash, piffle, claptrap, bunkum and tosh? You decide.

THUNDERSTORM, AMERICA, 1840s

In the USA, the railroads began to spread steadily west from the cities on the east coast. Then in 1849 there was a gold rush when gold was found in the far west, California. The 1849 miners were known as forty-niners. You may have heard the famous song about a miner's daughter, Clementine.

In a cavern, in a canyon,
Excavating for a mine.
Dwelt a miner forty-niner,
And his daughter,
Clementine.

Clementine, tripped on a splinter of wood, fell into a gushing river and drowned. (Don't cry, it's only a song.)

Settlers in the east were desperate to cross the prairies, the deserts and the mountains to get to California. Trains were needed to cross the continent.

But those railways to the west were built quickly and carelessly. There were many accidents building the railroads and riding on them. Only the brave or the greedy would head off into the wild west.

Rail workers were attacked by native tribes for days on end. Sometimes they were massacred and never seen again. But the strangest disappearing act was when a whole train vanished. Another ghostly tale? Or something a lot simpler?

A huge freight train from Kansas Pacific Company was rolling across the country in the 1860s when it drove into a thunderstorm. At the heart of the storm was a giant waterspout. It washed away a quarter mile of track in a blink.

The freight train was there when the waterspout struck. It could have been thrown into a gorge with a deep river at the bottom. Maybe it came off the track and was buried in deep sand. It has never been found.

VILE VILLAINS

Running a railway can make you money. George Stephenson died a rich man. He bought a fine house in Derbyshire and kept inventing things. But criminals can find ways to make money from railways too.

Tehachapi, USA, 1883

A train was standing at the platform when two strangers climbed on board. They unfastened carriages from the locomotive so it would steam off and leave them to rob the train.

But … they were on a slope and they broke the

link with the brakes when they unfastened the coaches. The carriages rolled down the hill, faster and faster till they came off the line. Fifteen people died. Two of those 15 were the rubbish robbers.

Medford, USA, 1888

Forcing a train to stop is a wrong – but not all train-stoppers are robbers.

At Medford, near Boston, USA, the train company refused to stop for the farmers of the little town … it would slow the whole journey.

There was a steep climb up to Medford and one day the express train driver found that his wheels began to slip. The train puffed to a stop. The villagers jumped onto the train. They had covered the tracks in slippery treacle.

The driver had to back up and take a fast run to get over the slope. And the villagers said they would cover the tracks in treacle every time they wanted to stop a train.

The villagers got the station they wanted.

England, 1867

A ticket collector watched a woman get on the train at the same time every day. She went to the next stop and came back on the next train. He was baffled, puzzled, perplexed and mystified. What was she up to?

Then one day she stumbled, and he saw six shoes shuffling along under her wide skirts. He couldn't lift her skirts up to check. Far too rude.

He sent for two women inspectors and the next day they took her to a waiting room and looked under the petticoats. There were two 4-year-old children hiding there in school uniform. She was their nanny. The parents paid

111

her to take the children to school. She bought one ticket – for herself – and saved the children's fares by sneaking them under her skirts.

People who dodged fares cost the railway companies many thousands of pounds. The fare-dodgers tried many ways to beat the inspectors. In 1849 passengers had to pay a lot of money to buy a ticket for a pet dog. One passenger told the tale...

1. Near Nottingham a woman got into the carriage carrying a heavy baby. It wore long clothes and a shawl over its head.

2. On the journey the child made a noise that was just like the barking of a dog.

3. An old lady, sighed: 'What a dreadful cold that child has got to be sure.'

4. The woman with the baby said, 'Yes, she's had the flu.'

5. At Nottingham, the ticket collector opened the door and shouted 'Tickets please!'

6. The sudden noise shocked the baby and it gave out a loud bark. The ticket collector pulled back the shawl and found that he was looking at a young Dachshund.

There's an old saying, 'Let sleeping dogs lie.' But the only lie came from the cheating woman.

Seymour, Indiana, 1866

John T Chapman was a preacher. He knew that local gold mines sent the gold on the railroad. He wanted his share.

John T picked six friends to help him. They took their horses and weapons to their hiding place, an old mine tunnel. When the train was due at midnight, they rode to a station nearby and climbed on board as the train pulled away.

Some of John T's gang climbed into the cab of the locomotive and told the driver where to stop. They reached a quarry and came to a halt. The gang started unloading the gold onto the horses they had waiting. In minutes America's first train robbery was over.

Now you want to know if they got away with it... and could YOU get away with it?

No. Because John T made a mistake. He began to spend the money – far more than a preacher should have. So did his six friends.

They were arrested and they told the law officers that the gold had been hidden away in shallow holes in the desert. The men went to prison for twenty years. Twenty years in prison but much of their gold was never recovered and still lies hidden where it was buried all those years ago.

Iowa, USA, 1873

The ruthless robber, Jesse James, decided to rob a gold train in Iowa. His gang loosened a piece of track so the locomotive came off the rails and fell into a ditch. The crash killed the driver.

When they opened the door to the gold wagon, they found only $2,000. The gang went through the train taking money and jewels from the passengers. For a little cash and a handful of jewels, the driver died.

Kakori, India, 1925

The gang that robbed the Kakori train were after money to pay for guns for their rebellion. They wanted the British rulers out of India. They decided that a good way to do this was to rob a train loaded with British money. Sadly, a passenger was killed as the rebels struggled with the guards. A month later all the robbers had been captured and they were hanged, along with 30 other rebels.

Rondout, USA, 1924

New inventions help train robbers come up with new plans. The biggest rail robbery in US history was the work of the 'Newton Boys', four Texas brothers who robbed at least sixty banks and six trains.

The thieves threw bottles of a sleeping gas into the windows of the carriages, then left with $3 million.

But a gang member had an accident and shot one of the Newton brothers several times. The villains were arrested when they went searching for a doctor.

But not all railway baddies were robbers with guns...

George Hudson (1800–1871)

George Hudson was a powerful man in York when he met George Stephenson in Whitby. The engineer told Hudson of his dream to build a railway line from London to Newcastle. Hudson said he could raise the money to make that happen. Of course, the line would have to pass through York.

But Hudson was greedy. He had a plan to make himself rich...

Hudson made a fortune but spent it all and ran out of cash. When people started asking for their money back, he couldn't pay, and he was locked away.

Charles Dickens hated Hudson for the way he cheated people.

I want to throw up my head and howl whenever I hear Mr Hudson's name.

But the members of parliament let Hudson get away with it. Why? Because THEY put money into the great railway plan and hoped they would make a fortune. Railways and greed go together like a loco and its tender.

AND SO DOES POVERTY

Many people killed themselves because Hudson lost their money.

Hudson's statue in York was not knocked down; instead, they just replaced the head with that of another man.

Hudson died penniless. But he was known as 'The Railway King'. Railways became great because of his great plans.

DID YOU KNOW...

Hudson's son, William, became a doctor. He died five years after his dad, The Railway King. Will was killed by a train.

EPILOGUE – WINNERS AND LOSERS

In the history of railways, YOU are the winner because you have a safe, fast way to travel around the country. There have been other winners.

WINNERS

1 Horses

In 1835 there had been 3,300 stagecoaches carrying 10 million passengers each year. As they raced each

other for business they wrecked the roads.
Coaches paid to use the roads. Those charges
were increased to pay for the damage and fares
went up for the passengers.

Horses were driven too hard, their lives shortened
so horse-costs went up. The railways were a stake
through the heart of the dying stagecoach industry.
Dick Turpin would have been cross. You can't shout
at a train the way you can at a coach...

Suffering horses were the winners.

2 Holiday towns

Factory workers in Britain used to get a week's
holiday each year. The trouble was they had
nowhere to go. If you worked in a Manchester
cotton mill you could walk 50 miles to Blackpool.
By the time you got there it was time to go home.

Railways changed that. Now special trains –
excursions – were run for the workers. Places like

Blackpool grew to keep the workers happy. In 1801 Blackpool had 473 people living there. By 1890 there were 35,000. Then in 1894 something new was added...

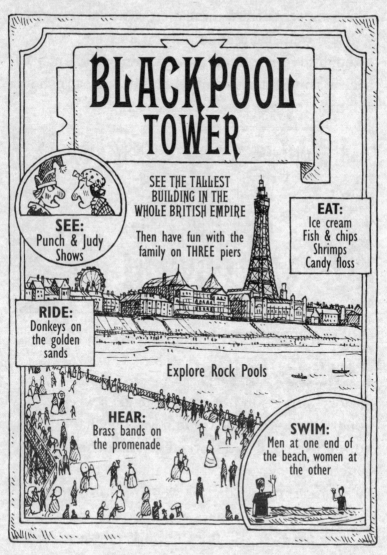

BLACKPOOL TOWER

SEE THE TALLEST BUILDING IN THE WHOLE BRITISH EMPIRE

Then have fun with the family on THREE piers

SEE: Punch & Judy Shows

EAT: Ice cream Fish & chips Shrimps Candy floss

RIDE: Donkeys on the golden sands

Explore Rock Pools

HEAR: Brass bands on the promenade

SWIM: Men at one end of the beach, women at the other

The first 'excursion' train was probably one run by the Bodmin Railway in Cornwall in June 1836. The same railway later took crowds of passengers on an excursion to see a public hanging.

Other excursions went to bare-knuckle fights, where boxers had been known to die.

Not everyone went to the seaside. In 1840 a special holiday train would take Sheffield families forty miles to Derby.

The excursion tickets were cheap but so were the carriages. A traveller from York to Newcastle in 1856 wrote to the newspaper...

York Herald

The train had four first-class, two second-class, and three third-class open carriages or tubs, which are only fit for carrying for pigs and sheep. Several of the passengers had tickets for covered carriages, but were forced into the open tubs by the railway company. They had to travel eighty-five miles on a wet night, open to all the harsh weather.

Many passengers made bleating or mooing noises like sheep or cattle to show how annoyed they were at being treated like animals.

Some crowded excursions took extra passengers on the carriage roofs and that led to awful accidents where heads argued with railway bridges … and lost.

A man on an 1849 trip from Preston to Liverpool dressed in his very best clothes for his day out. His clothes were stolen, and he had to travel home without a stitch.

Seaside towns and factory workers were the winners.

DID YOU KNOW...

The summer of 1916 was very hot on the East Coast of the USA. People took trains to the seaside and packed the beaches. Then they stopped. Four people were killed by shark attacks.

LOSERS

Great inventors made exciting new locomotives. Other engineers copied their inventions and made lots of money. The inventors never grew rich or famous.

Some brilliant, but forgotten, inventors were...

1 Nicolas Cugnot

Trevithick's engines were NOT the first steam vehicles in the world. A French engineer, Cugnot, had made a steam car in 1769, thirty years before him.

His machine flattened a wall, and he was arrested for dangerous driving.

THE FABULOUS FRENCH HAVE INVENTED THE CAR CRASH

The government gave him a pension. But twenty years later the French Revolution came along. The new rulers stopped paying the hero Cugnot. He ran away to Belgium and lived in poverty. Hero and loser. But a loser who made railways a winner.

2 Richard Trevithick

Richard Trevithick was one of the brilliant inventors.

At Coalbrookdale in Shropshire, Trevithick saw trucks pulled on iron rails (by ropes and a steam engine used to wind the rope). Trevithick put a high-pressure steam engine on wheels. There was an accident, and someone died. But Trevithick was a first.

In 1808 Dick Trevithick went on to put a high-pressure engine on a circular track in London and hoped people would order locomotives from him. He called it *Catch Me Who Can*.

But no one wanted to pay Richard for his locomotive. Earlier, in 1805, he had gone to Newcastle to build a steam locomotive for a coal mine. He must have met a young mine engineer called George Stephenson.

Richard was short of money, so in 1816 he went off to South America to build steam engines for flooded silver mines in Peru.

He came home in 1827 after an amazing journey more exciting than Treasure Island.

- He'd been forced to fight in a rebel army.
- He'd saved a lot of rich silver from his mines but had to leave them behind to escape.

- He had a little money left but was robbed of it.
- He made money by using his inventions to dive for a brass cannon from a sunken warship.

- He put the money into a pearl-fishing scheme in Panama … and lost it all again.
- Trevithick moved to Colombia, where he met Robert Stephenson, who was building a railway in that country.
- Stephenson gave Trevithick the money to pay for his journey back to England.

- When Trevithick arrived home, he found British engineers (like Robert's Dad, George) were using his steam locomotive ideas without paying him.

Four years later he fell ill and died in Kent. He was penniless and had no friends to go to his funeral.

Trevithick. Hero and loser. But a loser who made railways a winner.

3 Timothy Hackworth

George and Robert Stephenson made locomotives in Newcastle, but they were not very good. They were slow and kept breaking down. It was their manager, Timothy Hackworth, who had the job of getting them up to speed.

Timothy Hackworth worked for the Stephenson locomotive company and came up with ways to make the locomotives better than *Locomotion No.1*.

The engines on the Stockton and Darlington railway were forever breaking down. The owners of the line started to think horses would be better. But Timothy Hackworth said,

LET ME MAKE AN ENGINE *MY* WAY

George said, 'Yes,' and Tim came up with a new idea – the blast pipe. It made locomotives faster and stronger and they didn't fall apart every few miles.

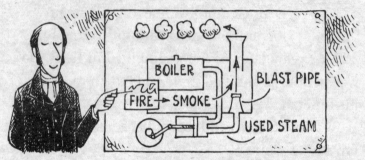

BOILER
FIRE → SMOKE
BLAST PIPE
USED STEAM

DID YOU KNOW...

George and Robert Stephenson were thrilled with Hackworth's inventions. They were so thrilled they did something unusual next. What?

A. THEY PAID TIM HACKWORTH DOUBLE WAGES

B. THEY STOLE THE BLAST-PIPE IDEA FROM HIM

Answer: (b) They took his idea.

Timothy was given the job of manager, but it wasn't a 'better job'. Daft Tim worked for a poor wage as the Stephensons grew rich. Hackworth had to work long hours into the night. A local paper said...

> **Mr Hackworth worked in weather frosty enough to freeze the wax as it ran down the candle sides.**

A writer explained...

George Stephenson is making lots of money and Hackworth is not; but Hackworth's locomotive designs are copied all over the world.

Tim Hackworth entered the Rainhill Trials to build engines for the Liverpool to Manchester line and make his fortune. He was so busy working for the Stephensons he had to have other companies making parts for his entry – *Sans Pareil*. But his locomotive sprang a leak from a valve and failed at the trial.

Who won the trial? The Stephensons and their Rocket.

Who made that useless valve that lost the trial for Hackworth? The Stephensons. A bit suspicious?

Timothy Hackworth. Hero and loser. But a loser who made railways a winner.

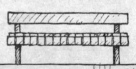

THE END OF THE LINE

Railways are getting faster, safer and more comfortable all the time.

But they are only safer because people in history made mistakes. Those people learned from the mistakes or they died. If they died, then someone else learned from them. People were crushed and burned, scalded and even atomised. Thanks to them you will not be crushed or burned, scalded or atomised.

That's what human beings do. They learn from the past.

Who would have guessed it? That history is so very useful? Especially Horrible History?

WILL IT GO KABOOM?

INTERESTING INDEX

Where will you find dreadful disasters, ghosts and hunting heads in an index? In a Horrible Histories book, of course!

TERRY DEARY

Terry Deary was born at a very early age, so long ago he can't remember. But his mother, who was there at the time, says he was born in Sunderland, north-east England, in 1946 – so it's not true that he writes all *Horrible Histories* from memory. At school he was a horrible child only interested in playing football and giving teachers a hard time. His history lessons were so boring and so badly taught, that he learned to loathe the subject. *Horrible Histories* is his revenge.

MARTIN BROWN

M artin Brown was born in Melbourne, on the proper side of the world. Ever since he can remember he's been drawing. His dad used to bring back huge sheets of paper from work and Martin would fill them with doodles and little figures. Then, quite suddenly, with food and water, he grew up, moved to the UK and found work doing what he's always wanted to do: drawing doodles and little figures.

COLLECT THEM ALL!

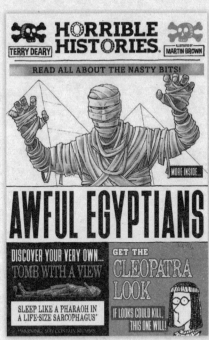

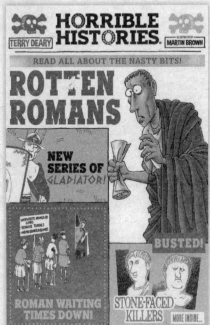

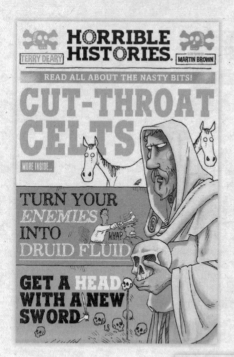

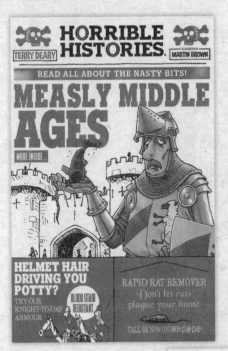

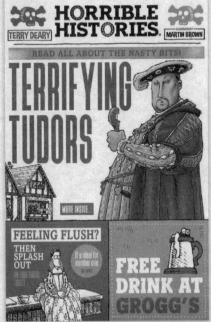

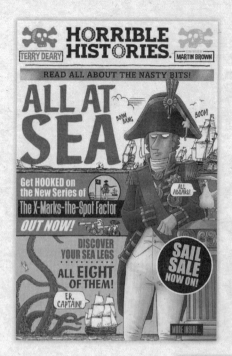